Family Time

Family Time

Peter Jaeger

Shearsman Books

First published in the United Kingdom in 2015 by
Shearsman Books
50 Westons Hill Drive
Emersons Green
BRISTOL
BS16 7DF

Shearsman Books Ltd Registered Office
30–31 St. James Place, Mangotsfield, Bristol BS16 9JB
(this address not for correspondence)

www.shearsman.com

ISBN 978-1-84861-452-9

Contents

Silas Flying

Silas understands the family way. And because he has been family since before families arose he remains family. Silas is high and broad, so the inconceivable power of soaring in the wind comes freely to him. A father said to his family: "children are always flying; the sky gives birth to clouds in the sunshine." You should examine in detail this quality of Silas flying. Silas flying is just like mountains flying. Accordingly, do not doubt Silas flying even though it does not look the same as mountains flying. The family also points to flying. This is fundamental understanding. You should penetrate these words. Because Silas flies, he is here. Although he flies more swiftly than the wind, someone in the clouds does not realize or understand his flying. "In the clouds" means the blossoming of the entire sky. People without sky cannot see how children fly. Those without eyes to see children cannot realize, understand, see, or hear this as it is. If you doubt children flying, you do not know your own flying; it is not that you do not fly, but that you do not know or understand your own flying. Since you do not know your own flying, you should try to understand how children fly. You should study children, using their numerous worlds as your standard. You should clearly examine children flying and your own flying. You should also examine flying backward and backward flying and investigate the fact that flying forward and backward has never stopped since the very moment before the family arose, which is exactly in the present. Keeping their own form, without changing body and mind, children always fly in every place. Don't slander them by saying they cannot fly. When your understanding is shallow, you doubt the phrase, "Children are flying." When your learning is immature, you are shocked by the words "flying children." Without fully understanding the word "flying," you drown in small views. Yet the characteristics of flying children manifest their form and life-force. There is Silas, there is flying, and there is a moment when clouds give birth. Because Silas is family, family appears in this way. Even if you see children as grass, trees, earth, rocks, or walls, do not take this view seriously or worry about it; it is not yet sky. It is a conditioned view. It is not the understanding of the family, but is just looking through a bamboo tube at the corner of the sky. Explaining and explaining is not agreeable to children. Set words and phrases are not the words of liberation. There is freedom in this understanding: "Children are always flying." You should study this in detail. There are boy clouds, girl clouds, non-boy clouds, and non-girl clouds. They are placed in the sky and under the earth and are called heavenly mud and earthly clouds. These clouds are explained in the ordinary world, but not many people actually know about them.

The Rurals / Ruckle Park

Hope is rising for the ovum finding this so fateful for our so clean firm gone damper with twilight.

Lake although the leafy spaces also laugh, wet and equalling an animal some fungi and a single cell a plant.

You won't remember limits but you'll swim instead enclosing flesh, turn around attached and glide whatever will be hands.

Head points down at first between the squatting leaves a leaflet slung in waters of a thousand high is low in union.

Float around a crust as anger is undone by trust becoming feet in the sac the pod announcing how our lives will hold.

Not-yet hair or scalp and nails the fossils in the garden equal muscles taut / it's all just one big muscle flex it with your empty hands.

Sorry but I've no idea what to call these leaves or fungi growing here between an amniotic sac and rattles of the chest is all.

Dissolve the stone between my ribs with breezes empty as the stone is anyway a magpie and the sunshine shadows of the ash split well for burning.

Long green lane where the crow won't fly and free range children play at trampolines and junipers and sky.

Flattens grass across the fields to where the tractor ruts of mud dry cracking in the wind above the sponges complex mammals and the birth blush of the briar.

That she would wish for onward tethers to a thousand cravings for example cucumber with peanut butter and the crumbs for feeding birds at noon.

How engorged and leaking how responding triggers all the streams and how the dog licks nettles from her paw and limps towards the stile / doesn't know.

For fetus—see foetus—we are now the clumsy ones and we must feed whatever undulates with pulse and breath and slowly swelling letters.

Lower your head to raise your hips then underneath grows darker in the pooling blood it puffs up simple forms of life survive and leave the ground in flight.

And the dangers of computers and cat poo and soft cheese and petrol and probably excitement with potatoes and the weeding of the garden in the sun.

Downwind hit by wind the grass and wool streams off the barbed wire fence and in our cottage how your belly swells out just below your stomach.

Solar winds bake fields above this village where the growth of a foot from buds cocooned inside releases waves they wash among / around yourself.

Prolonged in warm-blood mammals rural UFOs and muscles stiff from lessened lactic acids chlorophyll and elder stones.

In the yawning position, in the endless gliding and in the wind in the teeth like tiny buds appearing in iron fell to earth from space.

Stroll down skip we're wading through the husks and yellowed tufts the sun still churning fields and robins here with eyelids open.

Am I clotting this blood am I doing this right is there steam and gasses cooled to rain and do they understand your moods like me?

Muscle use and sharing deeper love of pine / how any part was fired up and open to the womb of plant-like shapes / their calves straight up and ankles clean.

Drink your folic acid lava pours out steaming congress mouths your name is what? or will be who more who than how.

Milk fed dawn asleep untroubled to be purple hexagons of cells they call them crystals of cholesterol.

To be born at the end of autumn, to be born when rafting, and you when you leave your raft it floats on things we shared (we shored).

Substance carries information to your cells to help them with their love until you're welcome home with us is you and we.

***

Maybe there for sea, wetter waves and no allusions: red bark, roots or windblown granite always moss where supine moss remains.

Foot on the rock by the sea and Silas wet from tides and salt—waves arrive, arriving waves again and also currents come in waves, swelling sea that he calls "sea."

Coast stretches cold pools, hard shells stick to darker shadows further from shore, barnacled in clumps and urchin cups, grey drains of salt lapping onto stone.

So cold the coast his happy molars growing in a row a brighter coast of teeth and tongue in harmony with our drawn "aw."

Wet toes curling west curling through floating weeds—where toes meet rock, rock surrenders to grey—splashed grey by the slow smell of salt.

Further out towards the otter morning. How salt clings wet to toes how we slept with mice, a tang of sea against his back-drip throat and spray.

How luck favours summer, steadies his hand—how rocks threaten me more than him, adding "rock" to his maybe twenty words.

He yawns from where his mouth shifts air he's outside too with fuller lips—they open onto teeth—learning to brush he sees me brush / so clean with wind Pacific fresh.

The tide a sheet held still by evening iridescence, low at dawn the islands fir-clad hills with dirty toes, thumping through the "slippy" rocks and un-named shells.

His index finger jabs and squirts anemones (those greenish bags) the tide still pulling out.

Dry his legs dry his bum so cold his back to turn and lift a foot to towel dry, dry his names they pull at grass and wheat with duff gone also dry his feet a waddled track.

So small the smaller leaf it crinkles down to crumbs and smaller wings.

Laughing in the lake for fish is here, a home that's almost here to work the almost always contact of his breath and tiny ribs expanding in the tent.

Water laps a generation follows rocks when ribs are waves in tandem with the inside / outside hope of whales.

When he hums hello or sleeping turns or when he sits within my arms, when slower moments turn or when salal still glisten wet beside the deer and "baby" deer still tear at leaves.

When there's no cloud, no boats—not even a wake—no shore to reach or "waves" when the ferry's horn announces simply nothing when he sleeps.

Index finger pointed at a "boat" or just his tummy pointing "baby" there inside his mom a brother / sister (Alma?) coming swollen belly cooler now with sun behind us all.

On the wisp of his hair above his ears or pointing still at dryer earth, at tangled wheat grass underfoot, the tidal pools and "rocks" (again today his favourite word).

Jumbled up and covered up with moss patinas, roots to lift a gentle foot and "stomp stomp / roar roar" in constant hum is all and every each in flight.

Cold on the feet so mucky he says "mucky" (saw this with my eyes at last) on green stone grey stone "twiddlers" with sauce and sand in his shoes.

Silas learns his up from down today but not quite sure of soft and rough repeating will (they say) protect his mind so rock / so sea / so tree is driftwood grey before or after log.

Ringing pee from his shoes in a tidal pool, the kelp all sizzling, broken crabs now "dead" he says another scuttles into shade.

How his mother never looks more clear than when her eyes turn sea, her arms turn out and up to sky or when he wakes in shade she's there.

In the clearing in the fog, clung to hills in his "eagles" or "moon" or "sand" washed to hummocks or the foghorn's *Om* on morning mist.

Food curls quickly down his August throat so brown and soft his chin and fingers wet with porridge then to sleep again.

How we're singing lullabies for fruit and how he also sings to all directions spreading out including shapes.

Shared Breath for Those at Home

6:48 most likely but possibly 6:38 EST
11:48 most likely but possibly 11:38 GMT

Family Time

7:36 Put some maple in here! **7:36** And the other reindeer? **8:04** You can have your croissant soon! **8:16** Wasn't that a dainty dish to set before the King? **8:21** It's not prickly you just go in there and there's space—lots of bits of space! **8:27** Mr. Popadom Egg Rodent! **8:27** She has snake hair! **8:47** Dad, look at this! **8:47** Dad! **8:48** I went all the way here! **8:48** Seriously! **8:48** Now you have to do this one! **8:48** That's easy for me! **8:49** I've got a cricket! **8:49** What? **8:49** I've got a cricket! **8:49** Where? **8:50** It's actually a fly! **8:50** Silas gave me the wallet to hold! **8:50** In my hand! **8:51** He has a little hole to break through! **8:51** That's him! **8:51** I think I should give him back to Silas! **8:51** Do you want to hold the guy? **8:52** Did you say yes? **8:52** You can put your hand like this and write! **8:52** Is he quite tickly? **8:53** Really tickly? **8:53** Can I hold him? **8:53** Now he's hurt! **8:53** Can we just let him go? **8:53** Because there was a leg broken off him! **8:55** Why can't you hold him! **8:55** Or we could put him in your glasses! **8:55** Put him in your hand and tell me if you want him! **8:55** Someone left a Lego box here! **8:56** Dad, I want to get on a swing! **8:56** I can do this backwards! **8:56** I'll show you! **8:57** Ready? **8:57** I'm hungry! **8:57** I already heard from Dad! **8:57** Dad: open! **8:58** Orange, strawberry, and apple! **8:58** And there's a new make! **8:58** There's one that's a new make! **8:58** Guess how many bear facts cards I've got? **8:59** Seven! **8:59** I've got seven! **8:59** I want to go on the monkey bars! **8:59** Silas! Silas jumped off this! **9:04** Both of the pens are like this! **9:04** This guy's a DJ! **9:04** Look at this! **9:05** I'm doing this piece as well! **9:06** He's got way big guitar! **9:06** You can put it in your wash bag! **9:06** It is for you only! **9:07** He has one shoe and one not shoe! **9:07** This is a really good DJ! **9:08** He plays the music! **9:09** And there's a DJ up here! **9:09** You won't even see his smile! **9:09** He's the dancer in the band! **9:09** He's the DJer! **9:09** In fact he's playing a disc now look! **9:10** It's written! **9:10** It says there it's written! **9:11** Cymbal! **9:11** He plays lots of drums! **9:12** I'm this guy! **9:12** There's three people here who are you?

9:12 Dad is the stereo Mom is the *guitarer*! **9:13** Who's that on my foot? **9:13** And then there's this guy in the corner called Sam! **9:13** I'm going to send this to Canada and say Happy Christmas to all! **9:14** Now I'm just showing you how to draw! **9:14** You all keep singing! **9:14** This is a guy who always has a bum here says Mr. Bumbum! **9:14** Actually I don't want to read a book I want some toast! **9:15** I'm still drawing this one! **9:15** Turns into a gun! **9:15** Is this one of your drawings? **9:25** It's a bumbum drawing! **9:15** I'm making a little boat thing so I can sit on! **9:15** I'm only having one of these cushions! **9:24** Ninja Hamster! **9:24** I'm a Ninja Hamster too! **9:24** *Draclia*! **9:24** Is Draclia scary? **9:25** Should I get your car keys? **9:25** No we can't walk up steps! **9:25** You can't get up! I'm going to get up! **9:36** Explodes! **9:36** Why don't we put that den away? **9:36** That den's yours, ok? **9:36** Yours is down there! **9:47** I'm nearly finished! I'll come in a minute! **9:51** Clap cause I singed the loveliest song! **9:51** Little silver beads! **9:51** I am the guard of the silver beads! **10:00** Sacky-sons dark man went to see a pig! **10:01** Nothing! **10:01** There! There! There! **10:02** There I am! **10:02** And that's a little ant! **10:06** Can you give me a challenge? **10:06** Give me a challenge! **10:06** What you writing? **10:06** Look what I can do! **10:07** Time how long it takes! **10:07** Do you have a timer? **10:07** Go! **10:07** How long did that take? **10:07** I know that guy in the stripey t-shirt! **10:07** Can you face me for ten times too? **10:08** Need to do five more! **10:08** Not comfy! **10:09** But not zipped up! **10:09** I'm a zombie! **10:09** I am a robot! **10:09** I was a robot! **10:09** Can you write "robot?" **10:10** My friend Hannah her sisters are her cousins! **10:10** Why do you keep writing what I'm saying? **10:10** I want to play with it—pretend writing! **10:11** I'm writing what I say! **10:11** Now I want to write "Alice!" **10:11** Can I sit in back? **10:11** Can I catapult it? **10:11** You catapult it on people's heads! **10:11** I'm a little skeleton! I love you! **10:12** I bang someone on the head! **10:12** I need my sword! **10:12** Have you seen my sword? **10:12** Where is it? **10:12** Little skeletons go! **10:13** I need my axe to go wham! **10:13** Wham on their head! **10:13** I will whack them in their heads! **10:13** So silly those skeletons! **10:13** Don't they have any good weapons? **10:15** You're good! As good as a monster! **10:16** Vicki and Grace have blue eyes! And I have blue eyes! **10:17** What's seven plus seven? **10:17** What's eight plus eight? **10:17** What's eleven? **10:18** See! **10:18** They both have the same dress! **10:10** That's not scary! **10:19** But that is a baddy's castle! **10:19** Probably the Zombie King! **10:19** I think it is! **10:20** Dashi's the name of Katie's cat! **10:21** Shall I put this up my sleeve? **10:22** My bullet! **10:22** I got your bullet still! **10:22** I was so tired! **10:22** I was sweating! **10:24** I really want short sleeves! **10:25** No, I go here! **10:36** We're ghosts! **10:36** Don't see us Dad! **10:36** Seriously can you not see us! **10:36** Dad I just need a wee! **10:52** Can I film? **10:53** Can I see? **10:53** And then, at the doctor's, this is what they told my dad to do, so he has to put this on his foot to get this *ginormous* splinter out! **10:53** Or else! **10:53** Uh, he's never seen it before, but if you want a close up we can show you! **10:53** So, it's quite bad, cause if he doesn't, if this doesn't work he has to go to A and E so it's quite a bad thing that he's got! **10:53** I want to help you! **10:54** Oh I've had that before! **10:54** I wanted to help you do this! **10:54** Can I see your foot? **10:54** So, this is, wait, I just need to show you! **10:54** That's it! **10:54** Oh! **10:54** He's gonna put this plaster on! **10:54** I need the magnifying glass! **10:54** Alma will press it down! **10:54** Don't touch his foot to too badly! **10:55** Oh yeah! **10:55** Great! This might work! **10:55** Let's hope it works! **10:55** Else he'll have to go to A and E's! **10:55** Now, next job! **10:55** I'll put this on! **10:55** You hold them together! **10:55** Silas does that! Can I do this? **10:55** I wanna do um the photos! **10:55** This isn't a photo I'm not taking! **10:55** Wait! **10:55** I need to take I need to film where we used! **10:56** So this is his drawer! **10:56** And these are his plasters! **10:56** Good Dad! **10:56** First he has to open! **10:56** I'll try and! **10:56** I'm not getting the film walking past! **10:56** We're gonna go to Sainsburys! **10:56** Why? **10:56** Can we go to Gloucester Road? **10:56** Can we look in some more charity shops? **10:57** Oh! **10:57** This guy is the photo of Dad! **10:57** When he puts this like that! **10:57** You can see! **10:57** So you might wanna take a little walk! **10:57** Uhh uhh! **10:57** Farting away and they farted into diorama monster's stinky mountain!

10:57 Yahoo baby Alma! **10:57** She is the superhero of farting contests! **10:57** Yeah baby! **10:57** He tries to wash his hands off 'cause he was merrily singing "Baa Baa have you any wool?" **10:58** Yes sir three bags full! One for master one for the Dave! **10:58** Turn! **10:58** No wait! **10:58** Wait! Wait! **10:58** Wait! **10:58** Oh I really need to go! **10:58** Done! **10:58** No don't do it! **10:59** Then, next page! **10:59** Wait! **10:59** What's on the other page? **10:59** Done! **10:59** Done! Done! **10:59** Oh yeah that page! **10:59** Done! **10:59** Do you have to do the words? **10:59** Turn the page! **10:59** Because then it's like a story! **10:59** Turn the page! **11:00** I want some toast! **11:01** I think a bee goes up my nose and it coughed me! **11:01** I need a poo it hurts! **11:03** It's a rainbow actually **11:03** Another colour! **11:03** Green I need! **11:03** That one! **11:03** Oh! **11:03** I want the really lovely one! **11:04** It's smelly! **11:04** It's smelly green! **11:04** I won't use this smelly green! **11:04** Orange girl—no, that one is mine! **11:05** Stink bum! **11:05** Smells like a stink bum! **11:05** Now I need another one! **11:05** No this one! **11:06** I'll give you a *huggle* but not a kiss! **11:06** Come to Toyland if you have a jumper and I do have a jumper on come in! **11:07** There is the skipping rope! **11:07** I need the skipping rope! **11:07** Up and down the dusty bluebells! **11:08** I bet your person's going to die in this one! **11:08** Chop your fingers off! **11:08** You're going to have to get used to being killed! **11:09** Look what you've got to go through! **11:09** Meow I am a Cheetah how do Cheetahs talk? **11:09** Not those ones the coloured ones! **11:09** A fish try with a fish one! **11:10** Those are mine! **11:10** When I've finished this! **11:10** What are you writing? **11:10** This is so tricky! **11:11** You've got to do it all again! **11:11** Up there and down there! **11:11** This is the scary bit! **11:11** I'm making an apple! **11:11** I made a apple! **11:12** I'm making a tiny apple! **11:12** What are you writing? **11:12** Who's that for? **11:22** Now I can't make my species, my onion-picket man! **11:22** Dad this is your computer remember? **11:25** Milky milky! **11:26** Moon! **11:27** More! **11:27** Mucky muckster! **11:27** Rock, rocks, slippy rocks! **11:27** Stomp! Stomp! Roar! Roar! **11:28** I want Mummy to do it! **11:29** *Twiddlers*! **11:30** I did make one for you with selo-tape and paper! **11:30**

And you're not there! **11:31** Has writing on it! **11:31** That's for your bedtime! **11:32** I'll show you! **11:40** This is my gun! This is my gun! **11:40** Let's fight then! **11:40** Should I? Should I? **11:40** I have to go to sleep now! **11:41** I sleep too! Then baddies come in the night! **11:41** We sleep with our swords! **11:41** No one gets me 'cause I'm the little girl! **11:41** Baddies in the night! **11:41** Here's a baddie on one ski! Smack him off! **11:42** It really hurts! **11:42** It really hurts me but it knocks me out! **11:50** By one by two my rifle is a new! **11:55** We're pretending we're dead and ill! **11:55** No I'm not dead I'm just ill! **11:55** You make me back into a princess! **11:55** I had to go on a big long search, didn't I? **11:56** I didn't find it, did I? **11:56** So you were dead forever! **11:56** Then they put a grave over you, didn't they! **12:00** I did put it in! **12:00** Now I'm going to cut she! **12:01** No Hopsey! **12:02** It's really tricky! **12:02** Quakety quack a boat to the ceiling! **12:03** Please may I have my scissors back? **12:07** He likes flowers! Everyone likes flowers! **12:07** Can I have a bit of your paper? **12:08** Where to? **12:25** Are you scared of she? **12:25** I did do floating! **12:25** I don't like you! **12:25** I poo on your head! **12:26** They put nails in him and then he died! **12:26** Can you get me one? **12:26** I do have knights! **12:26** Oh a horsie with wings! **12:26** Look: Indians, Americans! **12:27** Sword broken, shield broken! **12:27** Fairy fairy, deer man, fairy again! **12:28** Spiral! **12:28** I don't want to do that! **12:28** It's a spiral! **12:28** That's your writing page! **12:28** Can I write here? **12:29** Not writing anything just drawing something! **12:29** Actually I just want to do something in here! **12:40** Legoland! **12:50** Don't want you watching me! **12:50** Can I show you something with that? **12:51** Soup is coming soon! **12:52** Where is the bowl? **12:52** Don't get in! **12:52** Can you hand me a bowl what's in here? **13:00** La la la! **13:00** La la la! **13:00** La la la la rah rah rah! **13:01** It's quite annoying when that CD is on! **13:01** I'm doing a video! **13:01** Am I doing a video? **13:01** It's not a picture I'm videoing it! **13:01** Look! **13:01** It's a video! **13:01** Sing a song! **13:01** What a poo poo pah pah pah! **13:01** No! **13:01** OK Dad you sing a nice song! **13:01** Like "Baa Baa Black Sheep!" Just sing that! **13:01** Done! Lane! **13:01** I just eat the bottom bit then I suck it from the bottom! **13:02** Dad! Dad! **13:02** Done it! **13:02** Can I have some more water? **13:02** More water! **13:02** Don't want another picture! **13:02** Something in my guitar longer than this! **13:02** Wait! Stop! **13:02** If I was to stop! **13:03** Want some crisps! **13:03** I couldn't stop the box! **13:03** Are we nearly there? **13:03** Oopsa daisy couldn't get this one Dad! **13:03** I do! I do! I did a raspberry at them! **13:03** I did a raspberry at them! **13:04** I do a raspberry at them! **13:04** I did a raspberry at them! **13:04** Here you go! **13:04** You put it in your pocket! **13:04** I'll put it in your pocket! **13:04** I need a wee! **13:04** Cookies! **13:04** Cookie! **13:06** I need a plaster! **13:07** I was on a tree and I feel off and blood came on my hand and I need a plaster! **13:13** Look at that Poo! **13:23** For big big big! Everything that big is going to eat every dolly up! **13:24** That's mine! **13:24** Hedgehog goes in there! **13:24** Get the house all ready! Put him in! **13:25** Shall I put him in? **13:25** Drop him right there! **13:25** I dropped him! **13:26** Not too much dollies! No this is too much! This is enough! **13:26** Got enough dollies in! **13:26** Or else you'll be *squishified*! **13:27** How will I get through? **13:27** Never ever touch! Never hold that! **13:27** Going to kill me shout at me! **13:27** I love your dolly! **13:33** Oh my God! He has to take care of all of them! **13:37** F is for the S word! **13:43** I'm just getting a weenie mouse and the mouse can go on the rainbow! **13:43** Unless it's in the car or something in the back seat! **13:44** One of the baddies got dead and one got never to be seen again! **13:44** She's always working! I want to be a sleeper, a reader, and a kisser! **13:50** More! **13:52** Willy Wonka could be dead! **13:52** If Willy Wonka were here, he'd piss in our face! **14:08** Row row row your boat see you on the shore! **14:09** Send you back to the crocodile bay! **14:09** You're *ouching* me! **14:09** This is how you exercise your back! **14:10** Is that your yoga? **14:10** Do you have the monkey? **14:10** I'm not going to share my chair! **14:10** I'm going to snap you! **14:11** Finished! **14:12** I'm good at actually making bows on my picture 'cause I make a little scribble for a bow! **14:12** I don't know where it is so we chave to chooses the ones we did with the hopscotch ones! **14:13** I don't know where the other ones are! **14:13** That was where I put it! **14:13** I have to find pink! **14:14** And I'm drawing a little bit of pink down here! **14:14** My foot's getting hot! **14:14** Dad the ground's really hot! **14:15** Shall I draw another picture? **14:15** I need to get this bee wet again! **14:16** It's really good to get it off! **14:17** I did go to hey-diddle-diddle and there was real people! **14:29** I did a wee and a poo! I did one outside! **14:29** There's a slide at the lake! **14:30** Do they have a rocket in the Paris Dad? **14:59** No don't come in here this is my private place! **15:05** Be careful! Be very careful and very gentle! **15:05** You go in-head 'cause I'm the monster! **15:05** This is actually fast! **15:05** Now I can't do my fastest! **15:05** I'll hang off then! **15:05** Now I can't go my fastest! **15:05** Judges slog stop squabbling! **15:05** Look I know how to write something! **15:06** I know how to write "wow!" **15:06** I want to play chase! **15:06** 1, 2, 3! Who's pushing it? **15:06** Is this faster? **15:06** No you are not! **15:06** Yes I am! **15:07** No you are not! **15:07** Yes I am! **15:07** I am! **15:07** I don't believe you now! **15:07** Nincompoop! **15:07** I really want you to chase! **15:07** Ready ready! **15:07** Now I know why I keep getting it wrong! **15:07** Because! **15:07** Just leave it like that! **15:07** When you're done that one we'll have to set them out won't we! **15:08** I want to learn how to do starburst! **15:08** You have to pause them each time! **15:08** You have to pause them a lot of times! **15:08** It's funny that me and Alma are using the same colour! **15:08** When is he gonna get here? **15:08** Look! **15:08** This is crab! **15:08** Mom, do you know why it's different? **15:08** See the middle one! **15:08** I need the hook! **15:08** You can't just take it off someone! **15:08** Water! **15:08** Hello Mr. Sea! **15:13** No one needs jumpers unless you're very frustrated! **15:14** I say it for an hour then I get really angry about it! **15:15** I am bigger than you think! **15:15** No that's yours! **15:15** I do not need this there's not enough room it's not big enough! **15:16** What does that say? **15:16** Read what that says! **15:15** Read! **15:16** Read please! **15:17** Careful! **15:17** You're in the way! **15:17** Is that really a good secret door? **15:18** Look this is the real door! **15:19** Doesn't work oh yes! **15:19** Why is it very sharp? **15:19** Doesn't draw yes it does! **15:20** Done! **15:20** I will rip my page! **15:20** It's my page! **15:20** That one's my page! **15:20** You can have that page!

15:20 See there's that page! **15:21** I'm done with it! **15:21** Time to tidy up! **15:21** That's a book mark for you! **15:21** Don't ruin it! **15:21** Maybe I might leave this book up here! **15:30** When people feel ill you sing that Daddy song that makes them feel better! **15:43** What's a missle? **15:43** Could they kill people? **15:43** Why? **15:55** I got a million! **15:55** No one in the world can count to infinity! **15:56** When I bend my finger it hurts! **15:56** That nearly broke my finger off! **16:02** Hey I'm sleeping on the sofa this is my sleeping place where I'm sleeping! **16:02** No stop it! **16:04** You can be *Kraeger* and I will be *Chima*! **16:04** It would not be nice if you had blood all over your face! **16:05** Not Comfy! **16:07** No she might be a bit sad! **16:08** I'm taking my loom band necklace off! **16:08** Shall I get my wallet? **16:08** I'll give you some money because you don't have very much! **16:11** I'm learning to pour! **16:11** It's so high do you have longer arms? **16:13** *Ginormous* paw! **16:14** It can kill you! **16:14** Would you like if I made some punching mitts? **16:14** I'm doing a card for Grandpa! **16:15** I'm not having that one I want another one! **16:15** Is that what it actually says? **16:16** An hour, another hour, another hour, another hour, a half, a half, a half, another hour, an hour! **16:16** I don't need that one! **16:17** Now can you write something else? **16:17** When Mummy's not here can we watch Bugs Bunny? **16:17** Not on there! **16:18** Um a pencil for my birthday! **16:18** One of those lion ones what doesn't break! **16:18** Mine finishes there mine starts there! **16:18** Look you're just going to get stuck! **16:19** I just need to do something on it! **16:19** Everybody choose a colour for their name! **16:20** That thing's for Grandpa! **16:21** Babar goes to school the lion goes to school that one goes! **16:21** Babar goes to the other school! **16:21** No I have to rub something out! **16:21** We don't have any rubbers! **16:22** Cindy's got some rubbers! **16:22** Here's one! **16:22** I've got a monkey! **16:22** I'm making a pile of mazes! **16:22** Loads of them! **16:23** Shall I show you how you make really good mazes? **16:24** Just lost those three! **16:24** Breaks it more! **16:24** Still keeping it 'cause it's got a person on top! **16:25** Each person has to make a maze! **16:25** Whoever gets through first they're the winner whoever doesn't they're not the winner!

16:29 I need the weenie scissors! **16:29** Now can I do a bit more? **16:30** I can, I can! **16:30** No, I want loads! **16:48** Look how I can do! **16:49** Look how far my feet go down! **16:49** Look at my pretty legs! **16:49** I can't believe I can't reach! **16:57** Can you clap again! **16:57** Clap now! Clap now Dad! **16:58** Down like a lid! **16:58** A little little! **16:58** Time to attack you! **16:58** Will kill you! **16:58** You will get caught in a net with my soldiers in my net! **17:00** I can get in with my gun! **17:00** No I don't want any walls shoot down! **17:00** Now I have to sing my other song! **17:03** And don't lost it! **17:03** Look at my lovely picture! **17:04** No there's orange slices for me! **17:04** Dead! **17:10** Move yourself dance! **17:10** Move yourself dance! **17:10** Move yourself dance! **17:10** Move yourself dance! **17:10** Move yourself dance! **17:10** Move yourself dance! **17:10** Move yourself dance! **17:10** Move yourself dance! **17:10** Move yourself dance! **17:11** Move yourself dance! **17:11** Loom bands! **17:11** I unlock the box! **17:11** I wanna go with Mom! **17:11** I wanna do it! **17:11** This is the really tricky one! **17:11** You have to do it like this! **17:11** Everyday I think I've done two! **17:11** But I've just done one! **17:11** That's rubbish! **17:11** Can I see the side of that? **17:11** They're praying! **17:11** One's red, ones yellow! Move yourself dance! **17:11** Look how much yellow's done! **17:12** She's really good! **17:12** That! That! That! That! **17:12** Yellow's really down really good was it yellow? **17:12** Move yourself to dance! **17:13** You first have to wash my hands then you make dinner! **17:14** Now we put it in the bowls! **17:15** I want one like yours! **17:15** That your drying place? **17:16** The magnet's broken! Did you know that? **17:31** My feet are down there and my head is up there! **17:46** Are you keeping that in here? **17:46** No I want it so say "caterpillar!" **17:47** Anything else? **17:47** Can I have that? **17:47** Can I draw on the other side? **17:48** That says "Christmas is gone!" **17:48** Now it's my turn! **17:48** I do it! **17:48** Can I do it now? **17:49** My name is two and a half! **17:55** Otherwise he will chop my whole head off! **17:55** I'm a robot knight! **17:56** Because you're a knight, you save me! **17:56** The mission of the man is to slice the princess' head off! **18:04** We should get a whole handful of weapons! **18:05** This is our book! **18:05** Is this into a missile? **18:05** There we go! It's all packed up! **18:06** What missile about my whistle? **18:06** I am *Chima* and you're the king! **18:06** They got some rope! **18:06** And, they shoot! **18:06** That's your Batman suit! **18:07** We killed it with our missiles! **18:07** Kill him? **18:07** He's already killed! **18:07** He just comes back to life! **18:08** He's already killed! **18:08** My name's Leela your name's Ninja! **18:09** Mutant Ninja at your service! **18:09** Do you need any help? **18:09** On a swimming suit! **18:09** Don't get it! **18:09** I've got my mask and no one can see me! This is my mask! **18:10** Well it blinds you! **18:10** I'm eating a biscuit! **18:11** Hook! Hook! **18:11** This plaster is rubbish now! **18:12** I won't drive! **18:12** Ah, cool! **18:13** Do you want to go to Alma's Pirate Island? **18:13** It's for boys too! **18:14** What does that say? **18:14** Yeah it means like, like! **18:14** Here's my other *Spiderwick*! **18:14** Look how good I am at keeping the rally! **18:17** I have to get ready for bedtime ok? **18:17** Get out! **18:17** Get out please! **18:18** First I have to see if the dollies are alright ok? **18:18** Check the dollies are ok! **18:19** I look after all the ones in here! **18:19** Is she hungry? Is she starving? **18:19** Meow! Meow! **18:20** She's going to eat all the toys up! **18:20** O big bunny! **18:20** I love you dolly! **18:20** You're not, I haven't even got the bed ready! **18:20** I forgot the blankets! **18:21** Can you turn the lights off downstairs? **18:22** I did make a tower look how high my coolest tower is one two three four five six seven eight nine ten eleven fourteen sixteen eighteen fourteen eleventeen fourteen ten! **18:22** She doesn't teach me! **18:22** No she doesn't! **18:22** Now it's going to be wet! **18:23** I don't want to wash my hands! **18:23** Now it's getting all wet! **18:24** It's broken! **18:24** It is broken! **18:24** Well look! **18:24** I can't do it! **18:30** Mom shall I just put this up here? **18:30** I'll just put it near the bathroom door! **18:40** Well, we went on a brilliant cycle and it was quite amazing so um your turn to speak now! **18:40** Yeah tons and tons and tons it's all quite a lot of people and there was this big fair part like and it was only girls but racing! **18:40** And there was these fun fairs and like a drink at a café! **18:41** Something like that! **18:41** Well we had this cheesy thing and we had *um, um um* what's it called ginger beer! **18:41** And a crepe! **18:41** And we like and then we had ice cream! **18:52** It's not a home it's kind of like a forest in there! **18:52** It is a forest actually! **19:49** Brown! **19:50** Can you get Brown? **19:50** No one's allowed to see my picture! **19:50** Because it is very secret! **19:51** I can't reach it! **19:51** The pink's running out of ink! **19:51** I need two! **19:51** You're not allowed to look at my monster! **19:52** Well we don't know which kind of monster! **19:52** No one knows what kind! **19:52** Stop pushing my piece of paper! **19:52** You want to see what kind of monster? **19:53** I need them forever! **19:53** OK I'll put them in a pot! **19:54** You like my monster? **19:54** He was secret so nobody knew who he was! **19:54** If you look I'm not going to be your friend! **19:55** They'll only be allowed to see the other part! **19:55** You're putting purple on her belly! **19:55** You're putting purple on her neck! **19:56** Now I can't make my picture! **19:57** It's not very good! **19:57** It's too small! **19:56** It makes cracks! **19:56** I'll just have to do this rubbish ending! **19:57** I like skin on apple! **19:57** Mom doesn't know that! **19:57** This one's for sharing! **19:57** I only ate two! **19:57** Out! **19:58** Your other picture was brown! **19:58** And that one's green and brown! **19:59** You don't know what it is! **19:59** Tree! **19:59** No! **19:59** Well, I'm not going to be your friend! **19:59** Ok, it's a tree! **20:00** Told you! **20:00** Has to go there now! **20:00** I didn't put it there! **20:00** I put it there! **20:00** No I didn't put it there! **20:01** I saw that! It's blue all over! **20:01** Did you know what I was making? **20:01** Look at my guy! It's a monster with hair! **20:02** He got four but I only got three! **20:02** It's starry now! **20:02** This guy likes music! **20:02** This monster likes music! **20:03** I got a dragon too! And a tree! **20:03** Come with me! **20:03** You don't need to but it be quite nice favour! **20:04** I got this! **20:04** I've got this! **20:04** I've got this little bookie! Do you want to see? **20:04** Should we do that game when I do the head and you do the tail? **20:05** Do you want to play? **21:19** What can we do now? **21:19** I hate you because you're always away! **21:20** A good place is over there!

Alma Mala

Alma smiles periwinkle, apple Alma's voice, deer shield Alma sleeps and sleeps, milk and wool for Alma, Alma waking under wing, Alma sleeping early thorn, cumulous Alma's eyes, Alma lies in a lavender basket, bluebell Alma turns her head, Alma's dandelion sneeze, Alma bends her clover knees, damselfly Alma, Alma wren rain, Alma's smile quickens quince, little Alma looks at orange tips, rolled in her meadow brown Alma, brooklime Alma sleeps, Alma's talk a sip of milk, Alma's toes wrapped in wool, azalea cradles Alma, softrush Alma spreads her fingers, foxglove feeding Alma giggles, Alma's smile spring cleaning, straw-dot sunshine Alma squints, Alma grizzles alkanet, buttercup opens Alma's lips, carder bee Alma looks in my eyes, Alma's ringlet chin is wet, Alma are you pine with tears? bramble Alma waves her arm, Alma's hair spring grass, among sparrow's voices Alma's voice, moon sets Alma kicks, Alma's warm day and warmer milk, Alma snores a bee a noon, willow Alma lifts her head, Alma waggles alder arms, sapling Alma's laughter, Alma's eyes—blue twilight, Alma's milkcap grumbles, Alma's afternoon, under sedum Alma's hat, Alma rustles purple thorn, snowdrop Alma squirms, Alma stretches for vetch, Alma's primula gurgles, Alma dribbles daisy, Alma wriggles common blue, woollen Alma's cheeks, Alma murmurs rhododendron, sleeping Alma sneezes, rain gust Alma gush, cotton Alma's mustard spot, Alma curls in campion, clover Alma's cardigan, Alma's hair grown softer summer, magpie Alma turns her head, sage slinging Alma, rubbing ghee on Alma's cap, Alma yawns dotted clay, fine wool Alma, Alma comma Alma, Alma's selfheal scalp, Alma shifts her peony legs, first bath Alma floats, Alma wakes again again, midnight Alma's breath, sheepskin Alma rubs her wrist, Alma's cheeks grow rounder still, Alma's speckled wood, lavender smiles of Alma, Alma's hawthorn full of chatter, Alma sees sorrel, now Alma's done crying thistles, don't forget Alma's finch, Alma's ruby tummy, sunny Tuesday Alma's robin, Alma safe in siskin wind, lichen even Alma hears, Alma chatters juniper, Alma's goldcrest fern, Alma round on rowan, moon Alma warbler, Alma's sleeps beside a pearl, Alma's sleeping lady fern, woodrush Alma, cinnabar rain when Alma sleeps, pear for Alma's smile, sunlight Alma, Alma's plump forget-me-not, Alma nestles watercress, Alma's weekly birthday, Alma's clean bellflower, poplar Alma, common blue on Alma's basket, white plume Alma's chatter, Alma rolls her hands across the moss, Alma's beach eyes, sunshine Alma's tears, puffball Alma in my arms, parsley Alma sleeps again, Alma mumbles all night feathers, clouds this morning Alma laughs, willow Alma smiles, Alma turns to Silas laughing lilac, Alma's maple family, blueberry Alma's toes, Alma's honeysuckle home

Acknowledgements and Notes

Thanks to Ian Davidson for publishing an earlier version of 'The Rurals' in *English*, to Phil Davenport for publishing 'Alma Mala' in *This Dark Would: A New Language Art Anthology,* and to Karl Jirgins for publishing a short excerpt of 'Family Time' in *Rampike.*

Silas Flying adapts Dogen Zenji.

I wrote **The Rurals** when my partner Zoë was pregnant with Silas in Batcombe, Somerset, and **Ruckle Park** when she was pregnant with Alma on Salt Spring Island in Canada.

Shared Breath for Those at Home is for my family in Canada, and especially for my first son Julian who was born at 6:48 or perhaps 6:38 in the morning.

Family Time is collected from various notebooks.

Alma Mala – I was surprised to notice that my daughter's name Alma is an anagram of the word *Mala*, which is a string of 108 beads used in Buddhist and Hindu meditation—the poem consists of 108 very short meditations written during the first months of her life.

www.ingramcontent.com/pod-product-compliance
Ingram Content Group UK Ltd.
Pitfield, Milton Keynes, MK11 3LW, UK
UKHW041632190726
13854UKWH00006B/2455